Grandfather, E.J. Pout Snr, standing in a shoulder high crop of winter oats and beans at Kite Farm, Swalecliffe.

My Grandfather, E.J. Pout Snr, started farming with a small piece of land given to him by his father.

Besides his business interests Grandfather was a Justice of the Peace, council overseer, school manager and church warden. One of Kent's first farmers to drain the land mechanically, he bought his first set of Fowler steam plough engines and equipment in 1877. Six of his engines are recorded at The Museum of English Rural Life, Reading University. My Father, E.J. Pout Jnr, was a partner in the family farming business with four of his brothers. Grandfather in command; and together they farmed over two thousand acres breeding their own Shire and half Shire horses.

The farms were widespread and in order to keep in touch Grandfather, always an innovator, installed a private telephone line from Kite Farm to Frog's Island Farm, Herne, a distance of some five or six miles as the crow flies. There were very few telephones in those days but it was necessary, as Grandfather ran a complete farming enterprise including the blacksmith, carpenter's and wheelwright's shop, a steam mill for animal foodstuff, a chaff-cutter and a steam saw bench. After a full and active life Grandfather died in 1930 aged eighty years, leaving four daughters, five sons and twenty six grandchildren.

Grandfather's first set of John Fowler steam plough engines made in 1877. These engines were not named, but numbered 3364 and 3368.

Dr Keswick Bowes, our family doctor, on his way to Frogs Island Farm, Herne, Nr Herne Bay.

Before my father's marriage to Marguerite Bates in 1902 he was a member of the East Kent Yeomanry, a volunteer force comprising mainly of young farmers who provided their own mounts.

I ARRIVE AT FROGS ISLAND

On November 24th 1908, our family doctor, Dr Bowes, in his horsedrawn gig, was making his way along the Thornden Road heading for Frog's Island Farm just to check that old Mrs Ashby had everything tied up nicely. Mrs Ashby was the wife of one of Grandfather's oldest employees. She had brought many a son of the soil into the world, and many a daughter too.

She knew exactly what the opening remark would be when Doctor arrived, his sense of humour being tempered by country living! "Well, what is it this time? A spout or a gutter?"

I remember little of Frog's Island Farm, as I was only four when we moved to Greenhill Farm. Being just outside the town of Herne Bay, it was somewhat less isolated. Almost next door was a small private school run by two maiden sisters, the Misses Carey, and their mother, which I later attended.

Some recollections stay clearly in the mind and I recall the day when a small aeroplane came spluttering over the farmhouse with engine trouble and landed in the field opposite. I think half Herne Bay turned out to see it. So began the age of "Those Daring Young Men in their Flying Machines".

Greenhill Farm, Herne Bay, where we lived during the First World War.

1914 brought the first World War. To the farms came soldiers, horses, wagons and guns. Every available building and accommodation was requisitioned. Officers were billeted in the farmhouse and although they had their own batman, it involved a lot of extra work for my Mother and the domestic staff.

Many of the younger soldiers had never handled a horse in their lives and many of the young horses had never had a gun carriage rattling behind them. The result was often a bolting horse. We were, as children, on the alert for such dangers. Such an event occurred one Saturday morning when a runaway horse came dashing into the yard. We children sought sanctuary in the woodshed, slamming the bottom half of the door as the horse bolted past. The animal headed straight for the open back door, disappeared through the wash-house and ended up in the kitchen where Mother was in the middle of her baking. Making a hasty exit she raced upstairs, and called to us to stay where we were.

Peeping over the lower half of the door, we could see through the kitchen window opposite, the horse, firmly wedged between the table and the kitchen dresser which was laden with china. Looking somewhat alarmed, a white faced corporal was trailing a halter from a shaking hand, followed by a rather red faced sergeant, who appeared to be searching for a horse that had vanished into thin air. Help soon arrived and the great beast was gently eased out without doing much damage. Then came shrieks of laughter when it was discovered that in its fright the poor creature had left a large deposit amongst Mother's cooking!

The horse became wedged between the kitchen table and the dresser.

With many horses being commandeered, the 'Maid of Kent' helped to bring in the harvest.

As the war went on we made many friends among the soldiers. The farm was used as a staging post and as one regiment moved off to France, another would take its place. Some friendships were shortlived. We did not realize then that many of these young men would never return.

We children had our own junior army. Our badges and buttons varied slightly according to the regiment to which the donor belonged. My elder brother appointed himself Lieutenant, me a corporal and promoted his best friend to be sergeant over me! Even my sister as our Red Cross nurse failed to heal this little sore spot!

My younger brother was too young even to be a private and my other two sisters had yet to make their appearance.

We made our own toys. Presents were confined to Christmas and birthdays only and received no regular pocket money. Our toy cupboard had its share of home made planes. The models did not vary so much as the markings we painted on the wings. There were plenty of opportunities to study war planes. Many landed on our fields with engine trouble or because the pilots had lost their bearings. One misty day an aircraft landed in the long meadow at the rear of the farmhouse. We rushed out to see it. The pilot told my Mother afterwards, "You have no idea how relieved I was hearing children's voices speaking English. I was not sure which side of the Channel I had landed."

On bright moonlight nights we used to watch the Gotha bombers making their way to London and we also saw the occasional Zeppelin. When an anti-aircraft gun and searchlight were placed in a nearby field we had to stop this practice because of the danger of falling shrapnel. We then became shrapnel collectors instead. Apart from one large bomb which dropped at the rear of the house, the farm escaped unscathed and in fact very few bombs were dropped around Herne Bay.

• • • •

A pilot makes a forced landing in the mist at Greenhill Farm – we ran out to greet him.

The Land Army formed in the First World War to help out on the farms.

As war dragged on and on, the younger farmworkers were called to the colours and the workforce took on a new look. More and more women were entering agriculture. The food situation became serious and everyone who could lend a hand at harvest-time, did so. We children were given custard tins with a few pebbles inside to shake up and down, scaring the birds off, as we walked round the corn fields.

Had I been a little taller in those days I would no doubt have seen hundreds of little sparrows feasting themselves in the centre of the field, undisturbed!

Christmas was a time for family gatherings. Going away for Christmas was great fun especially when we went to visit our other Grandparents, John and Harriet Wiles, who farmed at Eastry near Sandwich. Most times we travelled in the wagonette but in rough, cold, wet weather we went in a farm van.

I think it was in 1917 we had a White Christmas and a white Christmas pudding. Despite the festive sprig of holly, the very few currants gave the pudding the appearance of a Spotted Dick. There was a great shortage of imported food and indeed, food in general. The rationing system in the second war was excellent compared to the distribution of food in the First World War.

Going away for Christmas was great fun.

Studd Farm on the Herne Bay to Whitstable road, where I spent the greater part of my youth.

Peace came at last and we moved to another of our farms, Studd Farm on the Whitstable – Herne Bay road.

There were many wanderers on the road following the war, mostly ex-service unemployed men with campaign medals and very little else. A farmhouse on a main road was an obvious call and my Mother never turned them away without a hot drink and a bite to eat.

I attended the village school at Swalecliffe. The Headmistress, Miss Hickman, was affectionately known as 'Molly'. She taught the children subjects which she thought would be fitting for the employments they would be most likely to undertake on leaving school. In most cases this would be farm work like their parents. Molly appreciated the need for adult education even in those days. Recognising my drawing ability, I was given the opportunity to draw the diagrams for her evening classes. First Aid interested me most. It was a chance to gain a little more knowledge of the human form. In the Spring of 1921 I learned that an appointment had been made for me to be interviewed by the Principal of Margate School of Art. So, at the age of thirteen and a half, I set off with specimens of my work, accompanied by Miss Hickman. Later, during the summer holiday a very official letter arrived stating that I had been awarded a full-time Art Scholarship.

Captain Harry Rowntree of The Artists' Rifles was billeted with my Eastry Grandparents during the First World War. He was a very successful illustrator and commercial artist and naturally my Grandmother showed him my early drawings. "Tell the boy to keep drawing from nature and one day he'll be an artist."

Thus encouraged I did keep drawing from nature and what wonderful opportunities I had with all the variety of animals which had the freedom of the farms and meadows, and the warmth and shelter in wintertime of those impressive thatched and timbered buildings.

This was a time when men who had laboured throughout the year could pause at the end of harvest, look upon stack yards full of neat corn ricks and truly feel that "All was safely gathered in".

High up in the thatched barn at Studd Farm it was fairly certain a pair of eyes was watching every move below. As a small boy I was just a little afraid of the beautiful barn owls which used to perch on the topmost timbers. As dusk approached they would begin hunting, silently swooping down among the corn ricks and farm buildings which later resounded with their hissing and screeching.

Eva Crofts, Laura Knight's sister, came to stay for a holiday. She also painted landscapes and portraits and allowed me to watch her at work. Whilst painting she would tell me what a struggle it had been for her sister to make a living at painting. This conversation had a great deal to do with the decision my parents took regarding my career a few years later. Laura Knight became a Royal Academician and was later created Dame of The British Empire.

The large thatched barn provided many a nights' shelter for the weary travellers.

Swalecliffe Church School where I attended at the time I was awarded a scholarship. Miss L.M. Hickman was headmistress in the twenties.

THE DAYS OF RABBIT HEAD PIE

During my life I have met many kind and helpful people. I must place Molly Hickman at the top of the list, for it was her efforts which launched me into the world of Art.

In the eighties, when one hears many moans and groans from parents and children, my thoughts go back to the twenties, or 'The Days of Rabbit Head Pie' as I like to recall them. Really difficult times for such as Old Nellie.

Nellie was a war widow, a proud hardworking woman with a young son, who took in washing and collected rabbit skins in order to provide for herself and the boy. I think even if there had been welfare assistance in those days Nellie's independent spirit would have refused it. Her small son, attending the village school, did not have the benefit of school meals or transport in those days and to children coming from outlying farms and cottages it could mean a walk of two or three miles in all weathers.

An example of Nellie's thrift was revealed one day when a ruler went missing in the classroom and the order to 'turn out satchels' was made. The teacher had hitherto admired the way that Nellie always seemed able to provide her son with a good sized meat pie, that is, until instead of a ruler a rabbit's skull was found in his satchel.

Nellie made full use of the skins she collected especially if the head had been left on.

Old Nellie taking home the washing and rabbit skins she had collected.

STARTING A FIVE YEAR SCHOLARSHIP

Very few scholarships were awarded then and most of the students were young ladies, daughters of feepaying professional men. Arriving on my first day I certainly felt the baby of the classroom. In fact I was the youngest pupil the school had ever had!

When day classes were finished we were then expected to stay for evening tuition as well. I could have been excused from this by reason of the long day I put in. Leaving home just after seven in the morning with a two mile cycle ride to the station to catch the train to Margate, and returning on the last train, to arrive home at ten o'clock at night. However, I had no intention of missing any lessons and I enjoyed the company of the older people who attended evening classes for the variety of subjects from handicrafts to life drawing.

In fact, as I was only fourteen, I had to have special permission to attend life drawing classes. This did not meet with approval by several elderly ladies and of course, rather shocked my aunts. "Fancy letting him draw nude ladies!" . . . "With nothing on at all?" Discipline was strict and I can honestly say that my young ears did not hear anything said out of place. When a young assistant Head, Mr A. Moody, was appointed his method of teaching was somewhat different from the rather old fashioned way we had been taught. He had little time for the middle aged ladies who seemed to take up more than their share of the Life room and no time at all for the lady who left blank paper where certain parts of the anatomy should have appeared. Taking her drawing in one hand and very dark pencil in the other, he proceeded to draw in every detail, saying "Students in my class draw what they see in front of them." This little incident led student and teacher to the Principal's Office. From that day onwards the difference of opinion between the Principal and his assistant was noticeable.

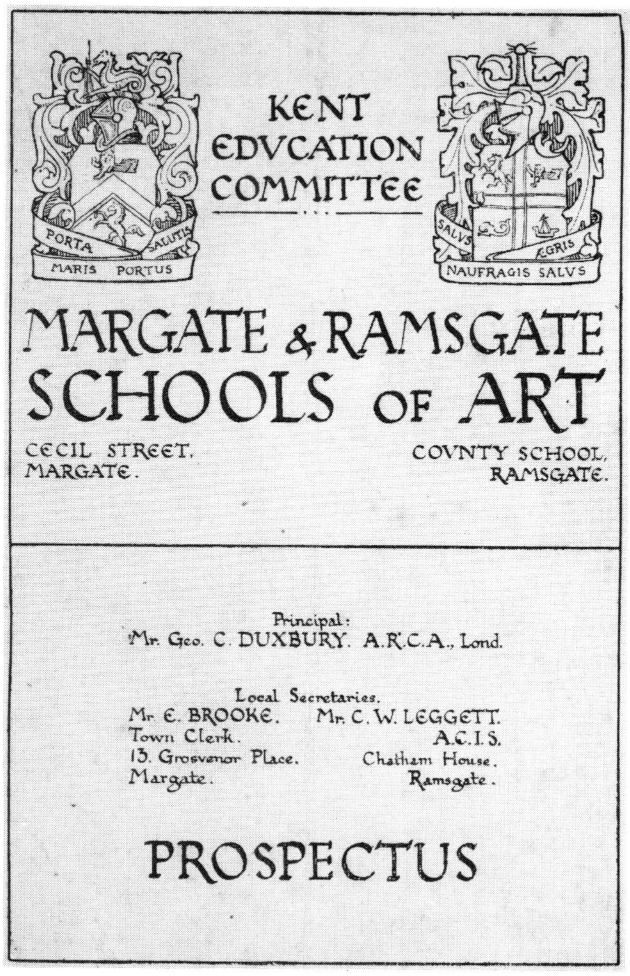

PORTA SALUTIS
MARIS PORTUS

KENT EDUCATION COMMITTEE

SALUS ÆGRIS
NAUFRAGIS SALUS

MARGATE & RAMSGATE SCHOOLS OF ART

CECIL STREET, MARGATE.

COUNTY SCHOOL, RAMSGATE.

Principal:
Mr. Geo. C. DUXBURY. A.R.C.A., Lond.

Local Secretaries.

Mr. E. BROOKE.	Mr. C. W. LEGGETT.
Town Clerk.	A.C.I.S.
13. Grosvenor Place.	Chatham House.
Margate.	Ramsgate.

PROSPECTUS

The Prospectus for Margate and Ramsgate Schools of Art, 1923-24.

Our Art School Annual Summer Outing usually took place at Fordwich on the river Stour.

Looking after these delightful little pigs and their Mums provided me with pocket money and the opportunity to carry on with my drawing during the summer holidays.

A REALISTIC OUTLOOK ON LIFE AND ART

The same young master persuaded me to change my original design for The Whitstable Horse Show poster. This was a young horseman holding a rearing white shire stallion. I was advised to adopt a modernist style which was becoming 'the thing' in the advertising world. Looking at that poster today – over fifty years later – I felt my first realistic approach would have been more acceptable to the Show committee, especially in those days.

With a shortage of males around, the younger girl students started to give me dancing lessons during the lunch hour in readiness for the Annual Art School Dance. I noted anxious glances between my parents as to where and what all this art school training would lead!

During the summer holidays I worked on the farm to earn myself some pocket money. Students had to provide and pay for all their drawing materials.

My favourite job was taking fourteen sows and over a hundred little piglets out on the grattons. I could sit down with my sketch book and try to capture the delightful antics of the little ones.

As I approached the age of sixteen and had attended art school for nearly two years, I was well beyond the usual age for children to leave school. Most of them left at fourteen to start work or become apprenticed. Art was not regarded as a trade or profession. The commercial aspect of it had yet to be fully recognised.

My parents, remembering the difficulties encountered by Laura Knight, and no doubt influenced by this, decided that I should leave art school and join the family business, regarding art as a hobby.

The Horse Show poster I designed which was ahead of its time – the organisers failed to understand the decorative treatment which was beginning to be used in commercial advertising.

One of my oil paintings showing the men enjoying their daily pint of beer at 'progger' time. 'Progger' mainly consisted of half a pound of cheese, the top of a cottage loaf and an onion.

TO BE A FARMER'S BOY

Although farming was in a depressed state like many other businesses at the time I got down to some physical and practical farming. I still have a very warm spot in my heart for all those grand old men who showed me how to tackle the various farming skills.

Our soil was heavy clay and the most practical way to do the Winter sowing was by hand thus I followed the six furrow ballance plough operated by the John Fowler steam plough engines Lord Kitchener and General French which were the second set of engines purchased by Grandfather in 1916.

I cannot remember the exact date of the issue of paper money but I do remember the disgust and mistrust with which the two pieces of printed paper, one a little smaller than the other, were met. After having a golden sovereign and a half sovereign in their wage packet, it was beyond the men's comprehension to be paid with paper instead of coin, for a fifty-two hour week!

Father and his brothers met every Friday night at Head Office to discuss business and collect the wages for their own group of workers. Father liked to walk rather than go by horse and trap and I often went with him for company. The journey home in wintertime could be dark and lonely, although wage snatches in those days were unheard of. The local Bobby knew every face in the village — a stranger would soon be noted. In fact anyone outside the village was regarded as a foreigner!

The local Bobby knew every face in the village.

The happy little caterpillar was determined to make the acquaintance of the wearer of that summer hat!

Swalecliffe Church, which is now surrounded with houses, at one time stood among the fields, isolated, apart from Swalecliffe Court Farm which has long since disappeared.

SUNDAY A DAY OF REST

Sunday was a day of rest. Only the care of the animals was undertaken. Waggoners would perhaps polish up their horse brasses and groom the horses and themselves, wander down to the 'local' and home to the Sunday joint. There were two services in church and Sunday School for the children. We were expected to attend church at least once on Sundays to set an example to the employees. Once, while sitting through a particularly tedious sermon, I felt an elbow giving me a gentle nudge. My elder sister's eyes directed my attention to the lady in the pew in front, who was wearing a large straw hat adorned with a huge bunch of artificial cherries. Leaping over the highly coloured fruit was one of those active little caterpillars, making his way rapidly to the edge of the brim and plainly determined to make the acquaintance of the wearer. Suppressing an outburst of giggles, it was not the wrath of God I feared but rather the stern eye of my Grandmother and Aunt, sitting upright on a well cushioned pew, specially reserved for senior members of the family.

The Maker of All Creatures Great and Small may well have been smiling down at the antics of this happy little fellow and wondering where He had gone wrong with some of the larger creatures.

I hope I have not given the impression that Grandmother was a tyrant. She expected good manners and respect.

During my lifetime my grandparents have been an inspiration to me and like the plants of the field, having deep roots has helped me to survive drought and frost.

Following the steam plough. Sowing by hand, eight to ten acres a day.

John Fowler engines, Lord Kitchener and General French, with their three wheel cultivator, caravan, balance plough, water and coal cart. These engines were the second set, purchased in 1916.

GOOD SERVANTS TO GOD AND MAN

The Keen family gave good service to our family for three generations, and to the village of Swalecliffe, too, as church wardens, bell ringers and organ pumpers. The sons, like their father, were mainly engine drivers. One acted as coachman when Grandmother decided to take a drive in her brougham. This was mainly when she wished to visit her children and grandchildren. Grandfather, on the other hand, was a great walker. He walked over the farms and not round them. That is the only way to farm properly. He was to remind my uncles of that fact when they decided to buy themselves motor cars!

When Grandfather walked the farms he did not just look – his walking stick had a spud fixed on the end and he jabbed out every thistle which dared to cross his path. At the end of a day stacking corn my hands bore witness to the fact that Grandfather was not winning, neither were the ladies who were employed to wander to and fro across the fields, in an effort to keep these prickly plants at bay.

'Cut a thistle in July and it's bound to die' is just another old saying or should I say just a little bit of rubbish. Of course the piece cut off will die – not so the root.

However, I believe that everything which grows on earth is here for a reason. What we as humans do not particularly like, may be food, or have some medicinal benefit for some other creatures. On our farms no chemicals for killing weeds or sprays were ever used. The steam plough engines with a three wheel cultivator would break up the soil and leave it fallow for a season, killing all the rubbish and giving the soil a rest. The rotation of crops was all important.

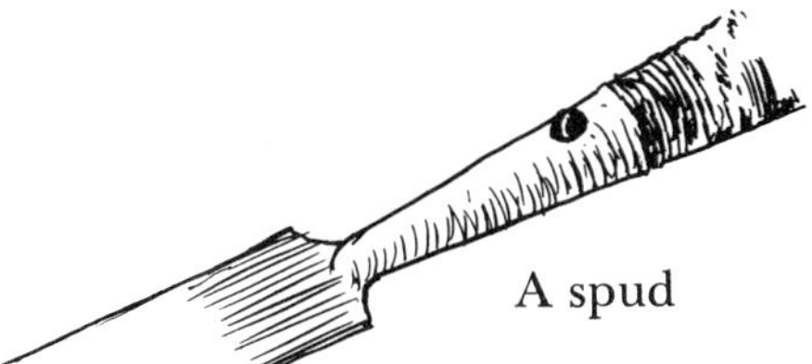

A spud

Grandfather spudding out thistles.

'Threshing in Kent', my favourite oil painting showing the 'Maid of Kent' threshing at Frogs Island Farm. Waddington Games have made a thousand piece jigsaw puzzle of this Kentish farm scene. Also Sharpes have reproduced it as a greeting card in their 'Gallery' collection.

FROM STEAM TO PETROL

When the Aveling and Porter steam engine 'Maid of Kent' after forty years service began to need a rest, we bought our first motor tractor, a twenty-five horse power Austin. The price was three hundred pounds.

On cold and frosty mornings, this tractor which started on petrol and then switched to paraffin was often reluctant to start. This was very frustrating for Earnest Keen driver and foreman of the threshing gang. The younger men took turns at swinging the handle, hoping the fiery little blue and red beast would spring into action.

What a contrast this was to the mornings when a little raking about in the firebox and a few shovels of coal would start the hand on the pressure gauge slowly moving up until the movement of the human hand set in motion that massive threshing machine. It produced a sweet humming sound which varied its note according to how well the corn was put through by the feeder. Another drawback to the Austin was that it was unable to position the thresher alongside the corn rick, especially when the ground was soft, in spite of the blacksmith making larger spade lugs which bolted through the plain flat surface of the wheels. As the Austin came hobbling across the stackyard she reminded me of a young lady trying to walk in very high heeled shoes.

I often thought when I saw the tractor boiling away with its rust stained radiator that Earnest Keen had not completely dispensed with steam. However this boiling little monster was to be short lived – import duties were removed and in came the Fordson tractor from America selling at half the price. Austin reduced his price drastically to £195 – the margin of profit was so small that production in England ceased but continued in France at their Laincourt factory just outside Paris until 1931.

The Fordson tractors were fast becoming a common sight on the farms – horses and waggoners were beginning to disappear.

On a cold morning she was reluctant to start.

The 'Pride of Kent' polluting the sweet air of Thanet.

POLLUTION IN THE TWENTIES

While attending a wedding a few years ago at Swalecliffe, I happened to see Fred Keen, a senior citizen, one time employee and driver of the 'Pride of Kent'. He was still carrying on his good work for the church.

I let him do most of the reminiscing. I was anxious to learn whether the glasses I wear when looking back are rose-tinted, as I have often been told they are. Fred talked about the 'good old days' for he genuinely believed they were.

Our conversation was bound to lead to steam engines as his father and two brothers were all employed as drivers. Fred went on to speak of that fateful day he was 'booked' for emitting excessive smoke. Apparently two rubber tyred Foden wagons, puffing out a lot of smoke in their effort to show their superiority, overtook our iron wheeled tractor, leaving in their wake a trail of pollution, the 'Pride of Kent', and a Bobby on a bicycle. The Law then overtook the slower moving tractor and brought it to a standstill and 'justice'!

Today with many drivers getting a ticket for parking or fines for minor motoring offences, little or no comment is made, but to have to attend court in the twenties was something of which a very law-abiding citizen like our Fred did not wish to be reminded, especially by his fellow drivers.

Our horses did their share of polluting but in those days small boys would be ready and waiting with shovels and handcarts for anything which happened to fall their way – and a keen gardener would be glad to pay up for the benefit of his rhubarb or roses.

Brothers Albert and Ted Keen with the Aveling and Porter light traction engine made at Rochester in 1912.

Biddenden Fair — 1973 was the last time there was a livestock sale at Biddenden. Over the years this annual sale and Fair has declined. An entry in the church register of a burial on December 4th 1709 reads — "A stranger. A Welsh drover as was supposed". Livestock was driven from many parts of the South of England to this annual sale.

MARKET DAY

Going to market in my youth was regarded as a day out and a very enjoyable one too, except perhaps the morning we drove fifteen bullocks from Swalecliffe to Canterbury market. We took to the road about five-thirty in the morning. By the time we reached our destination I was not sure whose feet had suffered most — mine or the animals. I noticed the bullocks made good use of the grass verge to walk on. My job, as the youngest drover was to go ahead and close any garden gates which may have been left open. By the time we reached Tyler Mill, the bullocks were fortunately tiring, otherwise I am sure they would have taken advantage of that long run down into Canterbury. We routed them as far as possible to avoid the shops, arriving before most city shop-keepers had opened their doors. It was window shopping only for our four-legged friends, until we finally came to the market entrance where carts and wagons lined up in readiness to unload their various cargoes. Today one would imagine that farm animals have a much more comfortable journey — but do they? Some cattle transport is badly designed. There is overcrowding and the handling of animals leaves much to be desired. Time and effort is put into improving farm output. I would like to see just a little more devoted to our livestock and the conditions in which they have to live in order that we survive.

"That's Cousin Henry. I'd know his shape anywhere!"

'The Blue Wagon'. The Royal Agricultural Benevolent Institute selected this painting to reproduce as their 1980 Christmas card.

THE BLUE WAGON

The blue wagon was a favourite of mine. Being a little lower and wider in the body, it was easier to load at harvest time.

This wagon was a stranger in Kent. Its colour alone gave away its county of origin – Sussex. I chose to feature it in my painting because the blue made a better contrast against the golden corn. Our Kentish wagons were mostly painted a creamy stone colour with red wheels. The Royal Agricultural Benevolent Institute selected the painting to be reproduced as their 1980 charity Christmas card.

Although the blue wagon wheels are no longer turning today, the cards carried good wishes to many people in this country and abroad.

Before leaving home in the early thirties, I re-lettered the name plate of wagon No. 21. While doing so, I was thinking of the hundreds of miles the wagon must have travelled carrying tons of foodstuff. But, as our carpenter was to remind us, there was little left of the original No. 21. There was no part that the carpenter and blacksmith between them could not replace to keep these wonderful wagons on the road.

• • • •

Over the years I have often thought how lucky I had been in my youth to have had the opportunity to watch these craftsmen carry out their various tasks, from the sawbench to the finished product.

After spending many hours of my spare time drawing this Rover Sports Saloon, the Rover Car Company informed me that this sports car was not very popular and they had decided to take it out of production.

2 LO CALLING

From a tall pear tree at Studd Farm, a pole could be seen sticking out of the topmost branches, with a wire leading into the house.

My elder brother had made our first crystal set.

There was an air of change or should I say strange things were coming over the air. We sat with earphones glued to our ears and tried to pinpoint that sensitive spot on the crystal. The coming of wireless brought a change in outlook and conversation to the farm worker. Gossip took second place to what they had heard on the set the night before: motor cars, new roads and young men leaving the land for more rewarding occupations.

"Men are like kittens – the sooner they are taken away from their mothers the better it is for them."

Thus remarked my Grandma Wiles. She felt that the farming family of Pouts with the third generation entering the business was getting too involved with family politics.

Grandma Wiles, in the late twenties, was a widow living in a bungalow adjoining one of our farms – near enough to keep an eye on this farming grandson.

In her early life she was governess and companion to the Dudley family. She had travelled with them and her conversation and the stories she told were most interesting.

Although we did not always agree on certain subjects, I had a high regard for her and I treasure a letter of encouragement she wrote to me in 1928.

I continued to draw in my spare time, mostly farm subjects but with an eye too on the fast cars which were beginning to take to our country roads. I spent hours on the coloured drawing of the Rover Sports saloon, only to learn that it was not a popular design and that production was to end. However they offered me employment at Coventry but I declined. I did not want to specialise in car drawings for advertising.

I have a letter dated 30.3.30 from C. Hardaker, editor of The Herne Bay Press, considering how best they could employ me, but meanwhile a journey to Dover was to solve that problem and bring a completely new way of life for me.

After a week of hard physical work I could relax with my sketch book on Sundays.

SUPER CINEMAS

When the super cinemas were built with luxury carpets and comfortable seats, they became the biggest entertainment attraction in most people's lives. Gone were the black and white 'flickers'. There was colour and sound, and organists like Reginald Dixon, Harold Ramsey and Sidney Torch were at the mighty electric organ. All these things combined made a very enjoyable evening out for just a few pence.

The Granada, Dover, was one such cinema and a visit I made in 1930 was suddenly to change my occupation and indeed, my way of life. On the front of the house were large hand painted portraits of the film stars, attractive displays in the foyer and panels with cut-out letters advertising the forthcoming programmes.

Here was art in an entirely new form. I think if the Principal of my art school had known that one of his past pupils was about to seek employment doing this rather low grade work, he would have been shocked and disappointed.

It seemed a fortunate coincidence that the East Kent Poster Service in Dover, who were supplying all this new type of cinema advertising, needed another artist. I started the following week. This firm were also printing by silk screen which meant that small numbers of posters could be economically printed with designs and simple illustrations, making them more attractive than plain typeset posters.

The Granada, Dover, Kent's first super cinema in the late twenties displayed on the front of house large cut-out heads of stars advertising the current showing of a film.

Preparing the press ads for the next week's big attraction.

A NEW LIFE

An entirely new life had opened before me, living in town and working indoors.

My art school method of working was far too slow. Speed was of the essence and there had to be a profit at the end of this artwork. There were no holidays with pay. We had to take a break when things were slack.

I had only been working at Dover for two years when I was offered a new job at Chatham, managing the Stoll art studios. I decided to accept, getting married at the same time to the girl I had known since my schooldays, Vida Standing, daughter of a neighbouring farmer.

At the Stoll studios, with five assistants, we carried out the complete advertising from press and posters to vestibule displays.

Some of the posters were so large that it was impossible to see them complete until the bill-posters had pasted them up. When an Act of Parliament was brought in, we ceased to produce many of the larger posters. It was against the law to put up advertising matter other than on approved sites and hoardings. Being involved with so much film work, I began to think how much more rewarding it would be if I could design the original posters for the film companies. To be a successful freelance artist one must be near the centre of work, London.

The top line of one of the larger hand painted posters which were replaced weekly, keeping my assistants busy. Also the bill posters pasting up hundreds of sheets on hoardings all over the Medway towns.

THE BATTLE OF THE MEDWAY POSTERS
Posters from 30 inches to 50 feet across

In the Thirties, three big cinema circuits fought it out. They were The Stoll, Gaumont British and ABC in opposition. Then came the Theatre Royal and Barnards Palace, both vaudeville houses. Top price at the former was eighteen pence. There was dancing at the Casino, Rochester, and boxing and wrestling as added attractions all fighting for the patronage of the Medway Towns.

Herbert Webster, who was at that time manager of Stoll's Empire Theatre, Chatham, had as his main opponents Don Shave at The Regent and Percy White at The Invicta.

Webster's strategic move was to form the Stoll Art Studios, producing posters, displays and general advertising, thus having an advantage over the other houses of entertainment. As well as a poster battle there were publicity street stunts, tie-ups with musical and record shops and thousands of hand bills and advance programmes giving details of the coming attractions, not to mention considerable press advertising.

THE CHATHAM EMPIRE

It seems almost unbelievable that this theatre had a staff of sixty. The staff were friendly and of smart appearance in their blue and gold uniforms. The manager and his assistant were in evening dress at the stroke of six each evening. The theatre bar was a very popular meeting place especially on Sunday evenings. Booking seats was advisable, price 1/6d or 2s. The theatre atmosphere was excellent. The large dome on the top of the building was on rollers and was moved back to allow all stale air and smoke to be drawn out.

The Stoll 'Wonder Screen' was also an attraction. When a panoramic view was about to be screened, the projectionist would buzz down to the stagehand who operated the shutters enlarging or reducing the size of the screen.

THE STOLL PICTURE HOUSE

The Picture House situated at the rear of the Empire Theatre catered for an entirely different class of audience. Comedy, Cartoons and Cowboys were the order of the day. Hundreds of Medway children enjoyed the Saturday morning matinees for just a few pence.

Mexican bandits ride the Medway towns advertising the film 'Viva Villa' showing at the Chatham Empire.

The Empire, Chatham. The commissionaire dressed as a Roman soldier during the screening of 'The Sign of the Cross'.

Above — a week before the showing of the film 'The Barretts of Wimpole Street' the above tableau was placed in the vestibule of the theatre, then removed to Jay's Furniture Stores and surrounded with period furniture, giving further publicity to the film during the week of showing.

Below — another street stunt which was pulled around the streets to advertise 'Hollywood Party'.

WARDOUR STREET, LONDON
The centre of the Film Industry

When a publicity manager was wanted to work in Wardour Street, I decided to apply for the post, although it was not altogether what I had in mind. Sometimes we have to take a roundabout way to arrive. Luckily I married a girl who did not seem to mind where my career might take me.

Now sitting in my office in Wardour Street, my new appointment was to be short-lived. Rumours of take-overs began to circulate. When they happened, many lost their jobs. I was offered a post as assistant to the publicity manager with a drop in salary. The thirties was not a time to be choosy with a wife and two small boys to support. My daughter was to be born a few years later during one of London's worst fire blitz in May 1941.

It was now a question of keeping one's eyes open for opportunities. A leading Fleet Street advertising agency required another general artist for their studio. I applied, although most of my work had been for film companies, and managed to get a foot in. I gained some valuable experience drawing advertisements for all sorts of products.

SCRAPERBOARD

Some very attractive results and a variety of effects can be obtained with this medium by scraping away the black surface with a sharp instrument and exposing the white clay coated card. All one needs is a very steady hand and a lot of patience. I found scraperboard was an ideal material where detail was required for advertisement drawings.

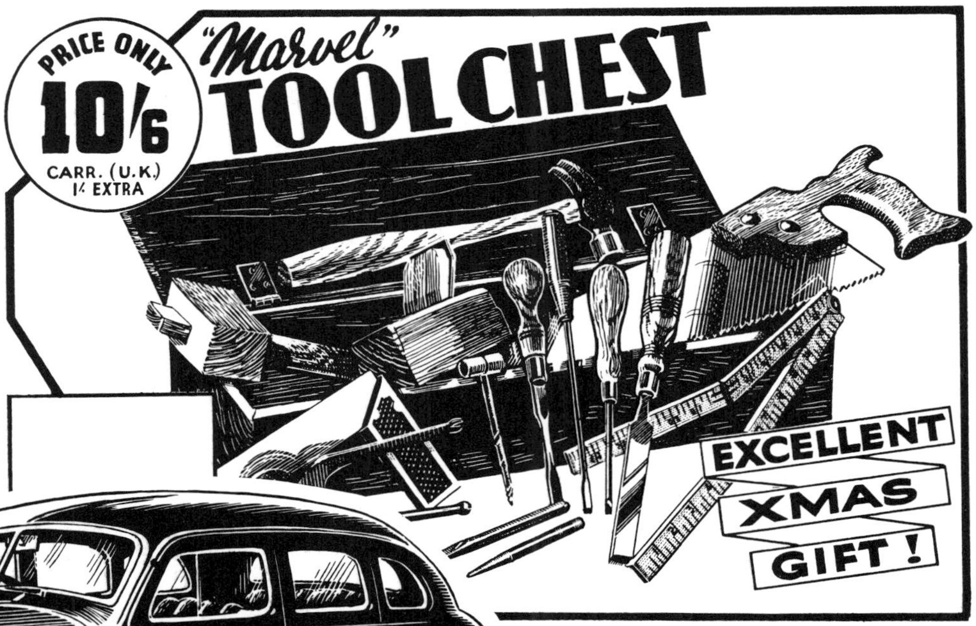

Just the figure of Charlie Chaplin was enough to draw attention to his latest film – 'City Lights'.

In the film 'Modern Times' Charlie found himself working in a factory. This gave me the idea of a caricature head made up of cog wheels.

Came 1938 and a crisis. We were all asked to take on some national service part time training and I joined the Metropolitan Police Reserve, training in the evenings at our local police station in Ealing and later taking a course at Peel House.

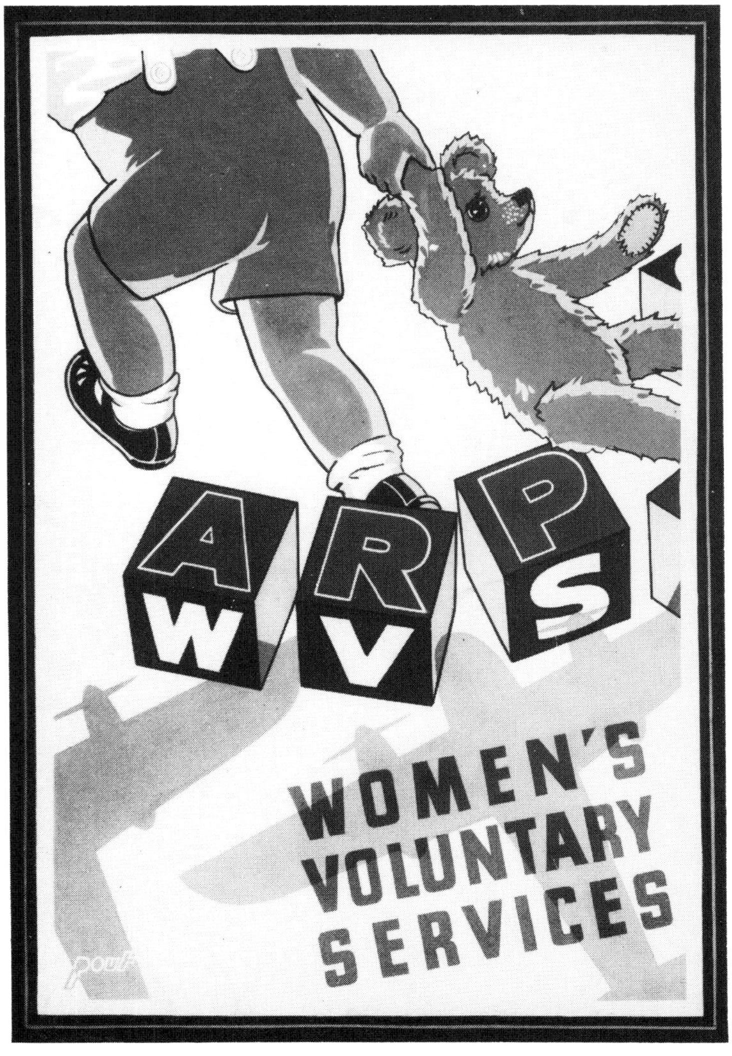

SECOND WORLD WAR

In September 1939 I was immediately called up for full time duty. It was threatened that half the police force and a great many civilians would be wiped out. Most of the children had been evacuated and my wife took the boys to Herne Bay and stayed with her parents. Nothing happened and the 'Phoney War' went on for several months.

We were released to go back to our civilian occupations. As my family were at Herne Bay, I rented a bungalow which was situated on the land opposite one of my old homes. The very land where I had sown corn for many years was now covered in houses and bungalows and a coastal road had been built, creating narrow strips of land between the road and railway line.

I travelled to Fleet Street every day by train and although it meant an early start to the day, I enjoyed my return to the country. It also meant a seat on the train instead of standing in a crowded tube train. In September 1940, bombing started in earnest and I was recalled to police duty. My wife wished us all to be together and so we returned to Ealing.

Unless the situation demanded otherwise, we did an eight-hour shift, early morning, afternoon and night duty. My weekly wage was £3. My agency did not make up my salary and my bank balance became smaller and smaller.

• • • •

Chosen as the best poster design from the Middlesex and London region in the A.R.P. competition.

Comedian Syd Walker, as a barrow boy, gave advice to BBC wartime listeners in the series 'What would you do, Chum?'

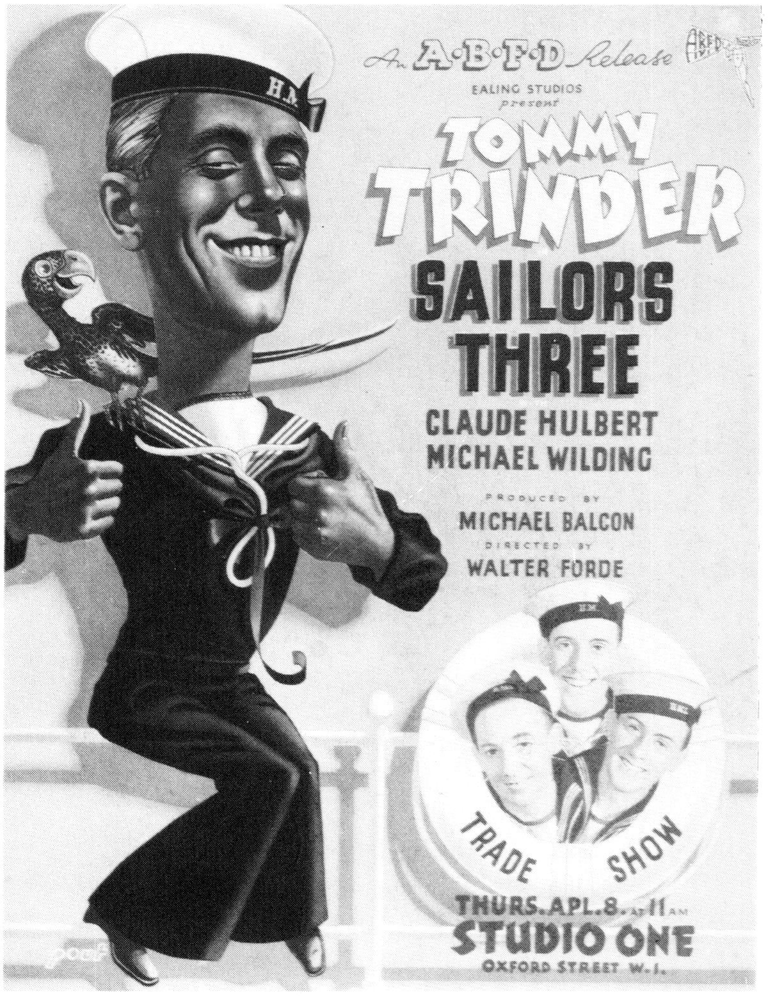

OPPORTUNITY IN SPITE OF HITLER

My experience in the film world enabled me to be of some use to the publicity manager of United Artists who introduced me to the late Sir Michael Balcon, the Ealing Studios Producer and other members of the Ealing crowd.

Here was an opportunity on my doorstep to design posters and press advertisements in my off-duty hours. It was drawing, duty and ducking when the bombs came too close for comfort. Soon I was designing the publicity for such films as, 'The Goose Steps Out', 'The Foreman Went to France', 'Went the Day Well', 'Black Sheep of Whitehall', and many more.

Tommy Trinder asked if I would paint a large caricature of him with his catch phrase "You lucky people". The crew of a bomber 'T' for 'Tommy' wanted it to stick on the fuselage of their aircraft. Having completed the job on a large piece of canvas, I made my way with difficulty to the West End through crowds who were already taking up their places on the underground platforms to shelter from the nightly bombing raids.

Tommy was playing at the London Palladium. The masterpiece was unrolled on the stage. "Lovely, lovely", exclaimed Tommy. I thought he was applauding as well, but as I turned I saw his hand was gently patting the bare thigh of the glamorous young lady at his side!

CREATING IDEAS FOR POSTERS

FILMS

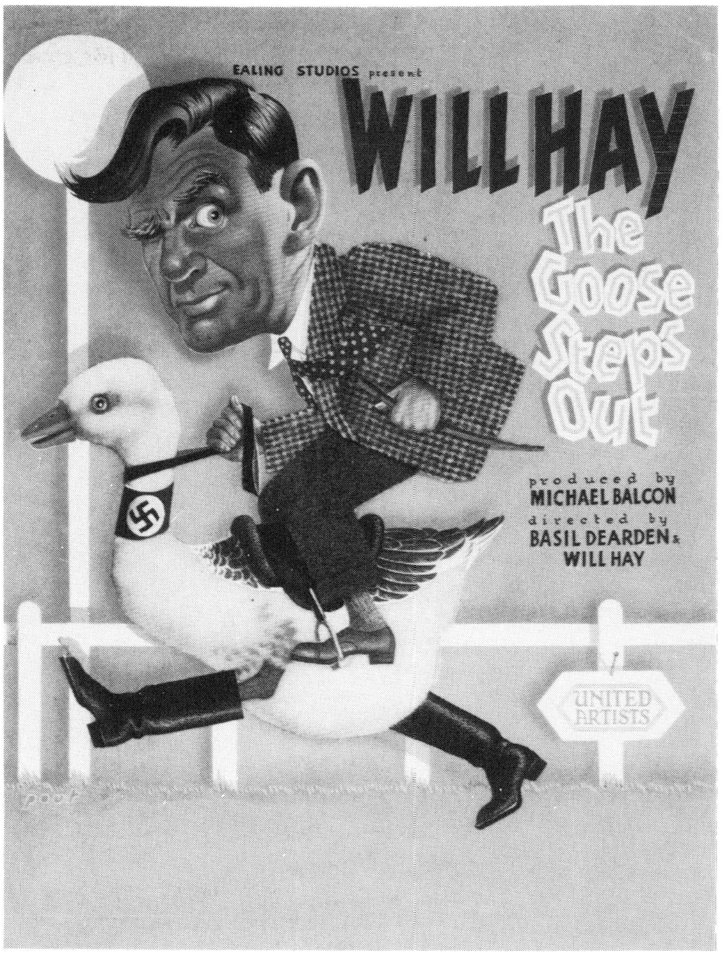

Before any ideas of drawing were put on paper, I would attend a private showing of the film, with the publicity manager of the company concerned. We would discuss what the best selling point of the film would be to feature on the posters. Correct billing was very important. The star or stars were placed above the title and the supporting cast were set below. Credits varied in size in relation to the importance and popularity of the star and were so much per cent of the title size, unlike today, as we see on television where credits are in alphabetical order.

Next came the question of how many colours were to be used, two, three or four. Every extra colour raised the cost of printing. After producing what is called a 'finished rough' and having it approved, the artwork was then completed. The lettering of titles, stars and credits was all done by hand. 'Rub down' lettering was unheard of in those days.

With the restriction on hoardings, the large 48 sheet posters soon became uneconomical to produce since very few cinema managers could find the necessary hoarding space in their area. Film posters have been on the decline for a number of years and we are now seeing the end of the cinema as a popular form of entertainment.

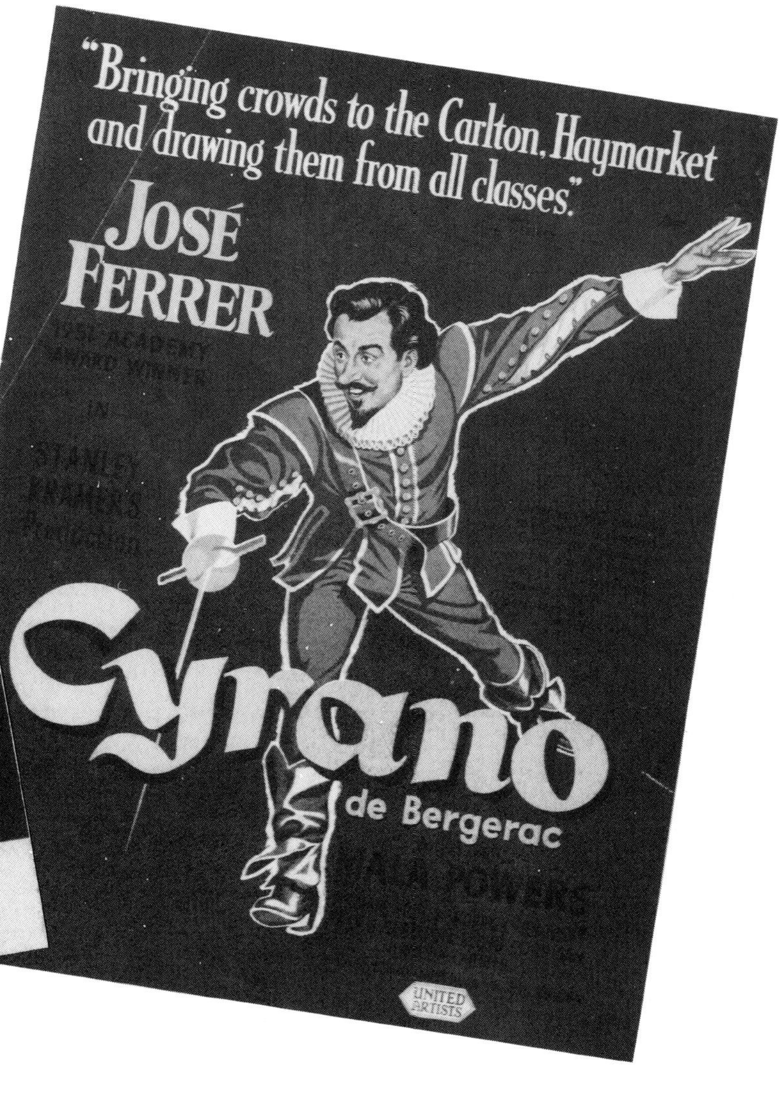

We had our share of unexploded and time bombs in Ealing. While standing guard over them, it was nice to have something to think of, such as an idea for the next Leader cover.

A PRESENT FROM HITLER

On police duty, when the sirens first sounded, we used to usher everyone into shelters. As the war dragged on the nation could no longer afford to come to a standstill with each air raid warning. Many carried on with their daily and nightly tasks. The bombing began to ease and we were just considering ourselves lucky when Hitler sent us a Doodle Bug. No doubt a present for all the cartoons and drawings I had done of him!

Having completed my night duty, I was trying to get some sleep. The blankets were well pulled over my head to lessen the noise of daytime activity. I woke suddenly in choking dust, part of the chimney stack in bed with me, roof timbers, bricks and slates all around and just a blue July sky above. Fortunately the children were playing under the Morrison shelter and only received minor cuts, but my wife was more seriously injured.

We were now without a home – with so many houses destroyed in London there was bound to be a shortage when war ended. I was still a serving police officer and had to live within the Metropolitan Police area. The V2s were still coming over but I took a chance and bought a property at Orpington.

With the end of the war in sight, I decided that I would not return to the advertising agency but would go all out to establish myself as a freelance artist. My wartime service as a London policeman was an experience which greatly enriched my life. I learned a lot about the behaviour of human beings in all sorts of situations and conditions.

Apart from the Columbia trade mark everything is drawn by hand including all of the lettering.

After drawing and colouring Rita's legs I covered them with net to give them a realistic finish.

Roy Rogers and Trigger the 'wonder horse' kept many children from the streets on Saturday mornings when special shows were put on by cinemas. Poor Trigger, now stuffed, stands in his own museum in Texas.

PATHE PICTURES LIMITED
PRESENTS
ROBERTSON HARE
ALFRED DRAYTON
IN
Ben Travers Famous Farce
Banana Ridge
with
ISABEL JEANS · ADELE DIXON · NOVA PILBEAM
PATRICK KINSELLA and VALENTINE DUNN
Pathe Gazette
PUBLIC NEWSREEL No. 1
An ASSOCIATED BRITISH PICTURE: Directed by WALTER C. MYCROFT
TRADE PRESENTATION: G.-B. THEATRE (FILM HSE.), TUES., FEB. 3, 2.30

A Riot of Love - Laughter & Larceny
Hear! Dick Haymes sing 'BELIEVE'
DICK HAYMES
NINA FOCH · ROLAND YOUNG
St Benny THE DIP
LIONEL STANDER
FREDDIE BARTHOLOMEW · OSCAR KARLWEIS
DIRECTED BY
EDGAR G. ULMER
PRODUCED BY
EDWARD J. DANZIGER
HARRY LEE DANZIGER
UNITED ARTISTS

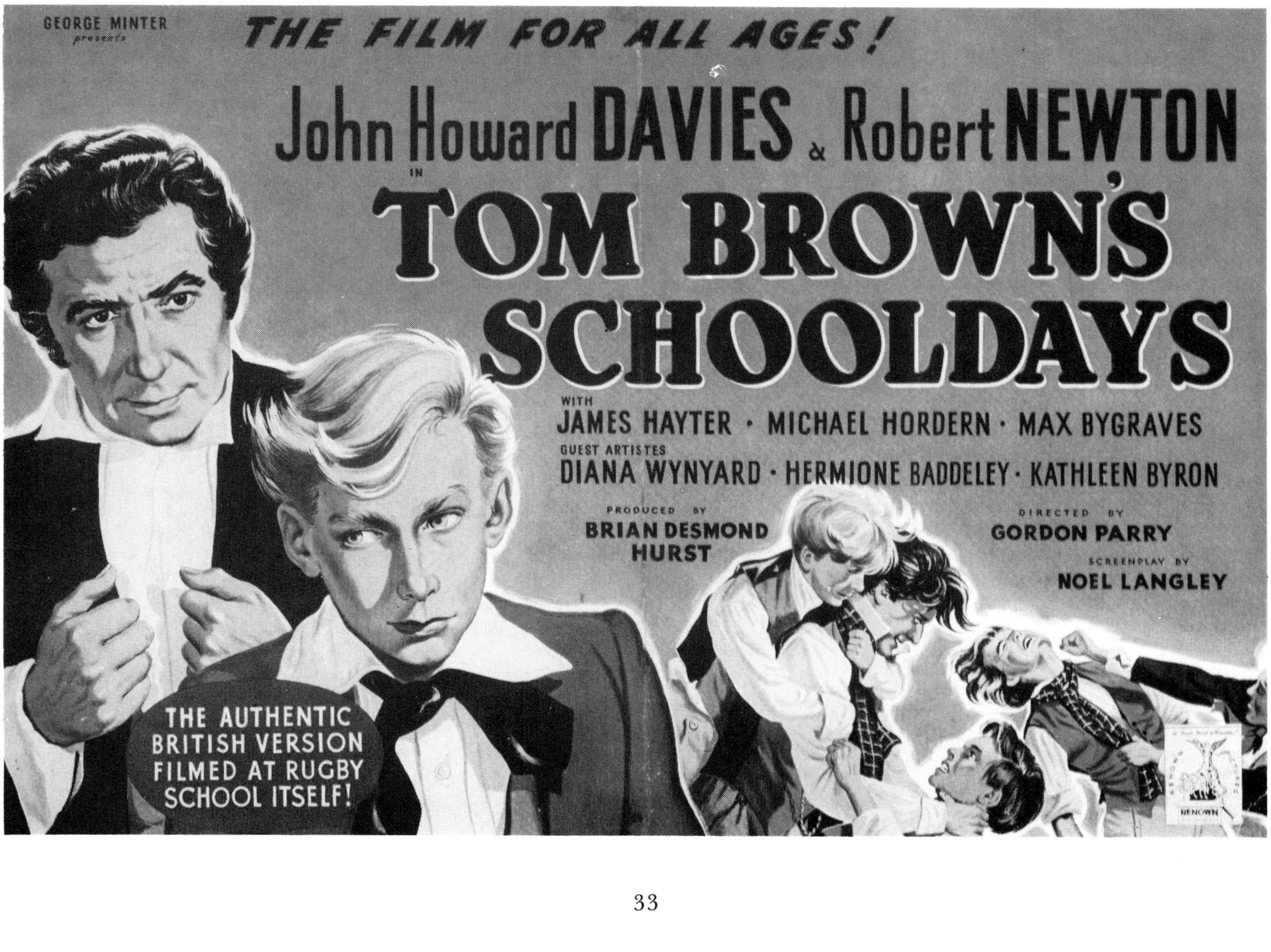
GEORGE MINTER presents
THE FILM FOR ALL AGES!
John Howard DAVIES & Robert NEWTON
IN
TOM BROWN'S SCHOOLDAYS
WITH
JAMES HAYTER · MICHAEL HORDERN · MAX BYGRAVES
GUEST ARTISTES
DIANA WYNYARD · HERMIONE BADDELEY · KATHLEEN BYRON
PRODUCED BY
BRIAN DESMOND HURST
DIRECTED BY
GORDON PARRY
SCREENPLAY BY
NOEL LANGLEY
THE AUTHENTIC BRITISH VERSION FILMED AT RUGBY SCHOOL ITSELF!
RENOWN

VICTORY AT LAST

With war at an end, it was simply marvellous to be able to remove the blackout, put the children safely in their beds and all get a proper night's sleep. It really was a wonderful feeling after all those years of darkness and terror to know that the only battle ahead was just to make a living.

My work was well known in Wardour Street, and commissions kept coming in but my friends in the industry were getting apprehensive. The outlook was not bright especially for the British film studios. In order that not all my eggs should be in one basket, I started to move into the publishing world. Drawing for magazines and the press, I was also a regular contributor to the most popular children's papers 'Eagle' and 'Girl', illustrating life stories and fiction.

Things were going well for us until my wife's health began to cause concern. We decided to move further out into the country and take a small farm at Biddenden. After several operations, my lifelong partner was to die, ten years later.

Bargate Farm Biddenden.

Eagle's 'Famous Persons' weekly picture puzzle.

Illustrating book jackets was not very well paid, especially if you had to wade through a story with little or no appeal just to find an idea for the cover. Magazine covers were mostly speculative. Today it seems all one needs is a pretty girl and a camera.

"Have you been drinking, Spellman?" asked Angus, pointedly.

"Swop me bob, I haven't, Padre—though I'm not saying I couldn't do with one!"

And again the man laughed. He was a tall, deep-chested fellow with a thatch of deep yellow hair and a heavy scrub on his chin. His eyes were blue and easy-going, his long lips were slightly turned with amusement. His soiled shirt lay open to his waist, and with his hands thrust indifferently into his trouser pockets, he

Illustrations by Dudley Pout

ANGUS struck Ben in the mouth, a blow so powerful and vicious that Ben staggered back with his arms spread wide

I was a regular contributor to 'Britannia and Eve', a magazine which has closed like many more in recent years.

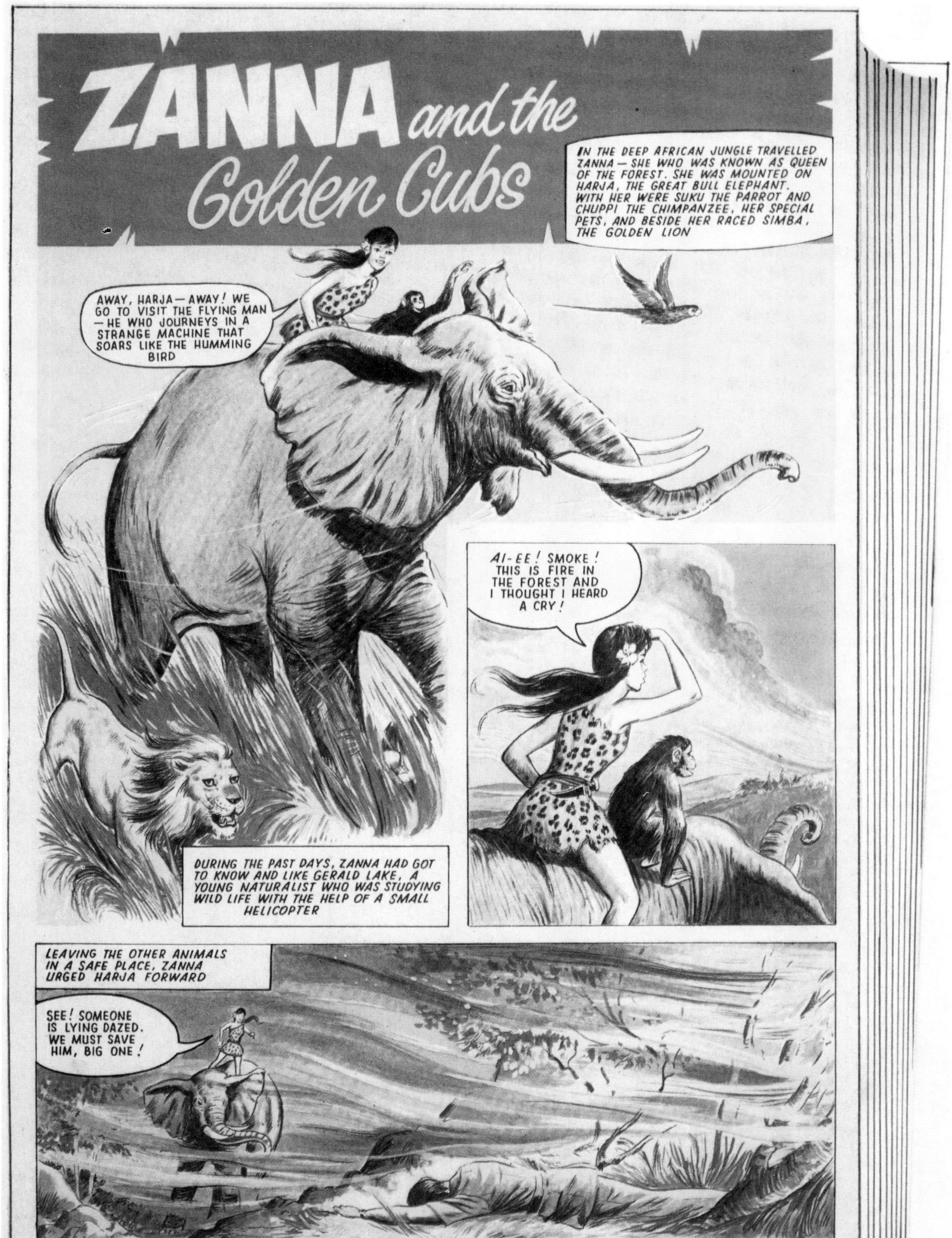

As well as work for weekly magazines, drawings were required for the Christmas Annuals, featuring favourite heroes and heroines. Zanna was another young lady whose adventures kept me busy with hundreds of illustrations for Fleetway Publications Ltd.

DRAWING FOR 'EAGLE' AND 'GIRL'

When I was asked if I would like to draw for a new type of childrens' paper and that well known writers and artists would be contributing, I decided to join the freelance group, illustrating historical, fictional and biographical material in continuity pictures.

We artists attended the Boys and Girls Exhibition at Olympia, signing autograph books and explaining how the art work for their papers was prepared. Because of the quality of the publication I found that the parents were just as interested and many were also reading the stories!

The Reverend Marcus Morris was Editor in Chief and the writers and artists spent many happy and rewarding years under his editorship, until we suffered yet another take-over and finally the papers went out of production.

'Angela Air Hostess' was a very popular story and continued for two years. Towards the end when it was thought that Angela might get involved with one of the married pilots, letters began to reach the editor's office from protesting mums.

Although history did not interest me at school, when the time came for me to illustrate the life of Mary Queen of Scots I found my self getting so engrossed with the story and costumes that I began to get behind with the drawing part.

The colour reproductions of the original drawings were excellent. Great care was taken by all artists to try and get everything as accurate as possible.

While I drew 'The Story of Amy Johnson' I recalled the days in the mid-twenties when Sir Alan Cobham, another world aviator, rented our land at Swalecliffe for one of his air 'circuses'.

'Esquire of Biddenden' my Aberdeen Angus bull at eighteen months old.

ENJOYING THE BEST OF TWO WORLDS

I bought some pedigree Aberdeen Angus in-calf heifers. It was a comfort to have solid ground under one's feet, and some nice looking animals to roam over the fields. The first heifer calved on Christmas Day. This untimely arrival just as I was about to enjoy my Christmas turkey, caused me to be absent for a while from the family feast. However this had its compensations later. The calf developed into a fine young bull, 'Esquire of Biddenden', and was purchased by the late Lord Plurenden. Esquire won many prizes at the County shows and came third at the Royal in 1965.

As the years went by I produced some good bullocks. These were sent to our farming group abattoir, where I was paid an extra penny a pound for quality beef! I felt this return was not sufficient, bearing in mind that Angus mature slowly. In the early sixties the French Charolais was introduced to this country. I was impressed with their growth rate records, and wished to put them to the test running them with my Angus, giving them exactly the same treatment. The claim about growth rate was quite justified but I was later to discover that their calving record left much to be desired. Losing two or three large calves and a cow with a calf weighing 120 lbs, made me begin to realise the so-called gain was becoming a loss. If only the Charolais calved as easily as the Angus . . . so I began to cross my Angus with the Charolais. The result was an animal which looked like a Charolais with a finer head and no horns. Although the Ministry licensed the bull, the Charolais Society, of which I was a member, refused to start a register for the progeny of this naturally polled animal.

My Charolais cross Angus steer won a first, a special and the Milk Marketing Board Challenge Cup at Wadhurst, Sussex, Fatstock Show in 1971.

ACTING MIDWIFE

On my knees, acting as midwife to one of my heifers, making sure that the calf was being presented in the correct position with its head nicely placed between its front legs, I heard a voice behind me say: "I'm not sure about you, Dudley. Are you a farmer or an artist first?" Well, I suppose to a number of people who may have been in one profession or job all their life I must seem to be a bit of a 'Jack of all trades' and then to complete that saying 'Master of none' could also be true. At seventy-four I'm still trying, and that is what makes life's journey so interesting. I have not set out to become an R.A. or 'master' of anything. The few simple lines on this page have brought a smile and even laughter. That is reward enough.

"Don't worry. Let him eat the lot – he will be the first to go!"

"Measles – nonsense! You're a young thrush!"

"Sorry I was not here to hold your hand, darling, but I was father to quite a number this morning."

Granddaughter Rosalind holding 'Boomerang', a five month old Murray Grey calf, sired by 'Bimbadeen Day Star', the first Australian bull to be imported by the Milk Marketing Board in 1973.

THE AUSTRALIAN MURRAY GREY

Reading in the farming press about my efforts to establish the polled Charolais, an Australian cattleman decided to call on me when he visited England. He suggested I might like their Murray Grey. These I have tried now for seven years. The young bulls I have sold going mainly to be run with heifers of a dairy breed, because of their good calving record. As most dairy farmers keep Friesians the popular bull for crossing must be the Hereford. There is no doubt about the ancestry of white face and socks when calves go to market. The Murray cross is not so easy to distinguish. When farmers buy calves they like a well matched bunch.

As a small breeder, the Milk Marketing Board's A.I. Service has given me chance to use top bulls, especially the Murray Grey bull, Willalooka Ambrose, which has never left its native Australia. In 1981 the M.M.B. carried out over fifty million inseminations. The success of this service to farmers speaks for itself.

A far cry indeed from my early days on the farm when the shorthorn bulls we kept had to oblige neighbouring farmers when their cows needed service. There was a health risk with cows coming in from a variety of farms. In the early seventies I was surprised to find a young lady inseminator had arrived to do the job – and very successful and efficient the girls are, too.

"If that's Daddy, how is it you have never met him Mum?"

My free range roadside stall. Not many passers-by took the word free out of context.

DEMAND FOR FREE RANGE EGGS

With many take-overs in the publishing world, journals and publications were disappearing. So were the jobs of many of my friends. These cuts had grave effects on the commercial artist and the illustrator. Television advertising was also draining the revenue away from the publishers main source of income.

I decided to increase my farm output by keeping some free range poultry. At this time there was a great outcry against the methods of factory farming.

Demand for free range eggs grew, so did my customers. The pullets I bred as replacements were not going to be enough. I placed an order by telephone for a quantity of point of lay pullets.

On their arrival I found that their beaks had been so severely cut back to avoid feather pecking in a confined space, that it would have been impossible for them to pick up food in the field. These birds had been reared in cages and were terrified of the great outdoors. They walked with a peculiar 'goosestep' gait. I am afraid they had to be returned to an imprisoned life.

While I was having a cup of coffee during one of my daughter's frequent visits, a representative called from one of the major poultry feed farms. "What are you going to try and sell me this morning?", I asked. "I'm not going to sell you anything," came the reply. "I've come to give you something – you have won our slogan contest!" Our coffee morning ended with something just a little stronger! Later we had an enjoyable day in London where the very likeable film and television comedienne Irene Handl presented me with The Golden Egg Reward. My free range enterprise had certainly shown a profit. But – and there is always a but, after a few years less and less was said about factory farming. I felt a number of housewives did not really concern themselves about the conditions under which the hens were kept, but rather more about paying those extra few pence for free range eggs which one must charge to cover labour costs.

As shorter and colder days approached and the hen's production naturally went down, I was forced to ration customers. They found it difficult to believe that the supply of eggs could not be constant and after I had explained the reason to one customer, she asked in the next breath, "Are there going to be any extra for Christmas?"!

Irene Handl seemed to be delighted with the gift of free range eggs and farm produce presented to her when I received The Golden Egg Award.

Grandson Mark feeding my free range hens.

BEHAVING LIKE ANIMALS?

How often have you heard the phrase: "They behaved like animals"? An Old Bailey judge made that remark when sentencing three men for rape. I have yet to see two male animals hold down a female while a third rapes her.

The poor old fox comes in for his share of criticism. "Kills for the sake of killing," it is said. Not true at all – man has collected, domesticated and bred birds, then shut them up in an enclosure. A hungry fox would be lacking in initiative not to take a fat imprisoned hen when it is offered. The other birds create such a fuss, he just has to silence them. Hens have had their natural defence instincts bred out of them. I have seen them almost waiting their turn to be annihilated. When a domestic chick strays from the hen it 'cheeps' loudly, drawing attention to would-be predators, but stumble across a pheasant and her chicks and the hen sits rigid, her chicks spread out like lightning, freeze and keep silent. I watched a cock pheasant draw the attention of a fox while his three hens moved swiftly through the grass, across the meadow and into the wood. What a marvellous performance the cock bird put on, waiting until the fox was within striking distance and then taking off like a 'jump jet'. The fox leapt about three feet, grabbing at thin air. "Kills for the sake of killing," they say and yet in his natural surroundings the fox does not have a second chance to kill.

Should the fox be hunted or regarded as a savage animal? During his lifetime he does less harm than man. When it is necessary to kill, he uses his teeth.

Biddenden Tea Towel.

In 1973 I retired to a smaller place surrounded by a Kentish vineyard at Biddenden. Keeping just one or two of my best cows, I intended not to accept any further commercial art commissions, but to start painting a few pictures in oils just for my own pleasure. I had settled down expecting to have a little time on my hands, when my neighbour discovered I was just the person to help with publicising his new winery, designing the labels for his wine, apple juice, cider, packaging and a tea towel.

Biddenden is a small village, and I was asked to design and make the village green centrepiece for the Jubilee Celebrations.

Then the famous Biddenden maids sign in the village centre required a face-lift! I support the Annual Art Exhibition and one year gave viewers a glimpse of some of my work which spans over fifty years, which included work I did for 'Eagle' and 'Girl' and many film posters which brought some nostalgic memories to older visitors.

My Biddenden postcards of bygone days, popular with the visitors.

Biddenden Village Green centrepiece for the Jubilee celebrations.

I was busy turning hay when Brian Johnston and his 'Down Your Way' team came to interview me. I had not met him face to face before and I found him an interesting and delightful person.

Following a half hour talk on Radio Medway, and last year a visit by Southern Television which gave our Art Exhibition a boost – what now?

Well, I have tried Murray Grey cattle for over seven years and now I have 'The Seven Year Itch', I intend to try and improve the fleshing on the British White Cattle, a dual purpose breed. All white with black muzzle and ears, they are reputed to be the descendants of the indigenous wild cattle from the Lancashire forests. I look forward to seeing these new faces in my farmyard and I hope to continue my oil paintings of the farming scene over half a century ago. Who could wish for a better way of spending one's retirement?

British White Cattle.